# Don Quixote

## Miguel de Cervantes

Academic Industries, Inc.
West Haven, Connecticut 06516

ISBN 0-88301-750-4

Published by
Academic Industries, Inc.
The Academic Building
Saw Mill Road
West Haven, Connecticut 06516

Printed in the United States of America

# about the author

The son of a doctor, Miguel de Cervantes was born in Spain in 1547. As a young man he joined the army and served as a soldier in Italy. There he was captured by the Moors and was later sold as a slave to a wealthy Greek. Somehow he won his freedom, but instead of turning to a quiet, happy life, he rejoined the Spanish army.

Between wars, Cervantes wrote his first novels. These brought him fame, but unfortunately very little money. As a result, he spent a good deal of time in debtor's prison—a place where people who cannot pay their bills are sent.

*Don Quixote* is thought to be Cervantes' best work. But as usual, though people knew its author, the book brought Cervantes no wealth, and he died penniless in 1616. This soldier, slave, and poet was one of Spain's most beloved writers, a man whose happy visions are as popular today as they were three centuries ago.

# Don Quixote

## Miguel de Cervantes

the mayor

the barber

Don Quixote

Rozinante

the housekeeper

Sancho Panza

In a village in Spain there lived a poor man named Alonso Quixano. One of the things he liked best was reading stories of the brave knights who lived long, long ago.

His niece would call him to dinner.

Uncle, won't you come to dinner?

Not while I'm reading about the great Knight of the Sun!

And his housekeeper would call him to bed.

Please, sir, won't you leave your books? You must get some sleep!

Not while the stars in the heavens call me to read these tales!

Day and night he spent reading stories.

"And so spoke Sir Amadis, The reason of your unreasonable reason so weakens my reason that. . . ."

In short, his brains had become a bit mixed up by these tales of long ago.

Often he would speak with his friends, the mayor and the barber, who also knew something about these stories.

Surely Sir Palmerin stands above all!

No, it must be Don Gandalin who is greatest!

Friends! How can you forget the Knight of the Blazing Sword who killed an army of giants with one hand? Could we but be like him!

Soon even these friends did not know what to think.

Where will it end?

Look at him! He thinks only of magic, giants, and battles.

9

But it was just beginning.

Enough of these books! I must become a knight errant!

He found his great grandfather's armor rusting in a forgotten corner.

Aha!

Carefully he cleaned it. For a week he worked until it shone like gold.

Surely it is as fine as any other!

*Then he went to the stable.*

Noble steed, forget that you were ever a simple horse. Now you are Rozinante, the mount of Don Quixote de la Mancha.

Now I have a wonderful name, fine armor, and a noble horse! But I must also give my heart to a beautiful girl!

It is well known, you know, that a loveless knight is like a tree without leaves, like a body without a soul!

It so happened that in the nearby village of El Toboso, there lived a simple country girl named Aldonza Lorenzo.

Of course! Aldonza will be my love!

Fairest of all maids, though you do not even know I love you, from this moment I give all the glory I may win to you alone. From this moment you are my fair Dulcinea del Toboso!

And so he rode off in search of glory.

Of course, it makes my heart sad to leave all this behind. But honor is all that is worth living for! And honor must be won by great deeds!

But soon he was struck by a thought that stopped him in his tracks.

Oh no! I've forgotten! How can I do great things when no one has dubbed me a knight?

Indeed it was so, but Don Quixote knew what he would do.

Hmm, I do believe I've read something about this. Ah yes, I must get the first person I see to make me a knight!

And so he rode on.

Ah, how happy the world will be when they read of my adventures! Surely they must read about them after someone wise has time enough to write of them!

But that day he met no one and had no adventures. Finally he grew tired and hungry.

*Soon he came to an inn.*

Look, Rozinante! We draw near to a castle, and two beautiful ladies have come out to welcome us.

*As it happened, a swineherd was just then blowing his horn to call his pigs.*

My good women, you must thank your noble lord for sounding the trumpets to welcome me!

*At that moment the innkeeper came out.*

Sir knight, you are most welcome, but we have no bed for you tonight.

I care not for a bed! I will sleep under the trees!

Well, then, I will stable your horse.

Indeed, take care of this fine steed! He is the finest piece of horseflesh in the land!

When the innkeeper returned, he heard a poem Don Quixote had just made up.

Never on earth was there a knight so well treated by ladies fair. Beautiful girls ran to serve him with speed, and a prince cared for good Don Quixote's steed.

Supper was brought to Don Quixote, but the women did not remove his helmet because he would not let them cut the ribbons. So they handfed him a bowl of smelly fish and moldy bread.

Ah, fresh trout!

As he ate, he thought about being a knight.

16

*The innkeeper grabbed him.*

But he tried to push me away! Doesn't he know that I must pray all night?

Stop that, sir!

Well, never mind. Let's get this over with.

But shouldn't we wait until dawn?

Oh, no. Times change. They got rid of that dawn thing a long time ago. In fact, rise, Don Quixote, and be gone quickly. The world out there needs you right away!

So Don Quixote prepared to leave.

Why, no. I've never heard of a knight needing it.

Say, do you have any money?

Well, now, that's a mistake. All knights carry a purse full of gold.

I didn't know that.

Take my word for it, you'd better go home and get some clean shirts too. And while you're at it, you'd better find a squire. Who ever heard of a knight without a squire?

19

And so Don Quixote headed back toward his village. But about dawn he heard screams.

What's that? It sounds like someone in need of a knight!

Hold, I say! Tis not right to attack one who cannot defend himself!

Sir knight, I hired this boy to watch my sheep, but every day he loses one. Now he wants to be paid so I'm paying him well!

Untie him at once and pay him, or I'll kill you myself!

Good sir, I will obey!

I am Don Quixote de la Mancha. I make wrongs right.

And so saying, he rode quickly away.

In a moment Don Quixote charged, but poor Rozinante stumbled.

Oh-h-h-h!

Then the mule drivers ran up to him and beat him badly.

They left him lying in the dust.

Rozinante! This is all your fault. I cannot get up, but no matter. I will sing!

22

The first song he thought of was a ballad.

Oh lady of my heart, do you weep for your knight?

Just then a man from his village happened to ride by.

What have we here?

Don Alonso, it is you!

I am not Don Alonso. I am Don Quixote de la Mancha! I have been hurt in battle with ten giants.

The good man did not know what to say. But he loaded Don Quixote onto his own animal and took him home.

That evening, the mayor and the barber came to speak to Don Quixote's housekeeper.

I just don't know what has become of him!

Look! Here he is now!

You must not read those books anymore! They have made you mad!

Then they carried him to his bed, and he fell fast asleep.

Fear not, good woman. The barber and I will take care of this while he sleeps!

*And so it was that Don Quixote was greeted by a strange sight when he awoke.*

What has happened?

Ah, an enchanter came on a cloud last night. He took away the books and the library.

Great magic stands in my way, but nothing will keep me from my job!

*For two weeks Don Quixote stayed peacefully at home. He spoke often to a poor neighbor of his named Sancho Panza.*

As my squire, you'll probably become very rich. Perhaps you'll even be the governor of an island someday.

Me? A governor!

25

He also quietly sold a few family treasures.

You mustn't tell my niece or my house-keeper. I need this money for impor-tant secret work!

Fear not, Don Alonso— I mean Don Quixote. Your secret is safe with me.

And so one night Don Quixote rode off again. This time, as the inn-keeper had told him, he had Sancho as his squire. He also had a sack of gold and some clean shirts.

The next morning they came upon many windmills.

Fortune is guiding us well! I will fight with these giants. Their riches will be ours!

What giants?

Why, those giants over there with the huge arms.

Take care, sir. Those are windmills, and what seems like arms are their sails which turn the millstones!

*Just then a breeze came along, and the sails began to turn.*

It is clear that you have not had many adventures! Look, they are waving their arms to try to scare me.

*Don Quixote attacked.*

Fear not! I will win in the end!

Sancho helped his master back onto Rozinante, and they rode on. They spent that night under some trees.

Master, won't you have something to eat or drink?

No, Sancho. I am fasting while I think of my true love, Dulcinea del Toboso.

The next morning Don Quixote fixed his broken lance with a branch from one of the trees.

Let us hope they will be better than yesterday's were.

There! Now we are ready to seek new adventures.

Then, while Don Quixote went over to the coach, Sancho Panza ran to the fallen monk.

At last! The rewards from my master's brave deeds fall into my hands!

However, the monk's servants ran to help him.

Take that, you robber!

You thief!

Meanwhile, Don Quixote had reached the coach.

You must be joking!

You have been rescued by Don Quixote de la Mancha. I ask only that you go to my lady Dulcinea del Toboso and tell her how you were saved by her brave knight.

33

So they rode on.

It makes me sad to lose my helmet. But I suppose it is worth it.

Better to lose your helmet than your head!

As night fell, they came upon the camp of some shepherds.

You are welcome to share our supper and our fire.

Many thanks. It is always an honor to visit people who live close to nature.

*Sancho didn't waste a minute filling his belly with the shepherds' stew. Don Quixote, however, wanted only a drop of wine so that he could sing about nature.*

When everyone knows of such joy as we share tonight, then truly we will live and be happy.

Just then another shepherd appeared.

What's this? Tell us more!

Friends, I bring sad news! Good Chrysostom is dead. He died from a broken heart given to him by the girl Marcela!

Ah, stranger, it's a story well known in these parts. The beautiful Marcela wanders with her flocks in the mountains nearby. All the men who see her lose their hearts to her. But no one can tame her, and many die like poor Chrysostom.

He will be buried in the morning, by the rock where he first saw her.

I must go there with you.

And so the next morning they all traveled to the rock.

Here lies Chrysostom. He loved Marcela, but he was hated in return. That girl led poor Chrysostom to his death.

She brought him to an early death as surely as if she had thrown him from this rock where first he saw her!

Suddenly Marcela herself appeared!

Be quiet! I have come to defend myself!

Some of the shepherds tried to follow her, but Don Quixote stepped forward.

Let no man follow! She has shown that she has little or no blame in Chrysostom's death. Indeed, she should be honored, not chased!

As soon as the funeral was over. . . .

Why have we left so soon, Master? Where are we going?

I must find Marcela and offer to protect her!

So they rode toward the mountains, but they never found the lovely young girl again.

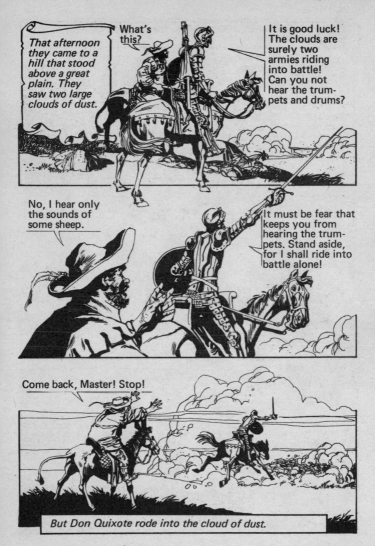

That afternoon they came to a hill that stood above a great plain. They saw two large clouds of dust.

What's this?

It is good luck! The clouds are surely two armies riding into battle! Can you not hear the trumpets and drums?

No, I hear only the sounds of some sheep.

It must be fear that keeps you from hearing the trumpets. Stand aside, for I shall ride into battle alone!

Come back, Master! Stop!

But Don Quixote rode into the cloud of dust.

39

In a few minutes he had wounded some sheep. The young shepherds ran up with their slingshots.

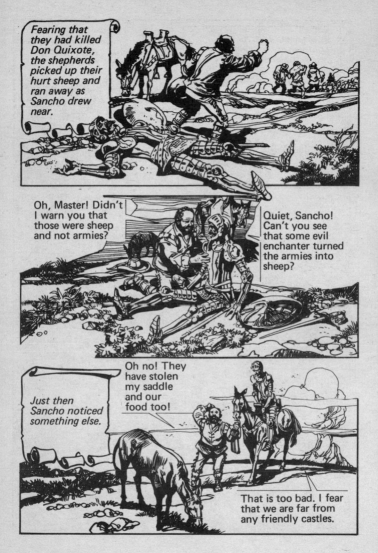

Fearing that they had killed Don Quixote, the shepherds picked up their hurt sheep and ran away as Sancho drew near.

Oh, Master! Didn't I warn you that those were sheep and not armies?

Quiet, Sancho! Can't you see that some evil enchanter turned the armies into sheep?

Just then Sancho noticed something else.

Oh no! They have stolen my saddle and our food too!

That is too bad. I fear that we are far from any friendly castles.

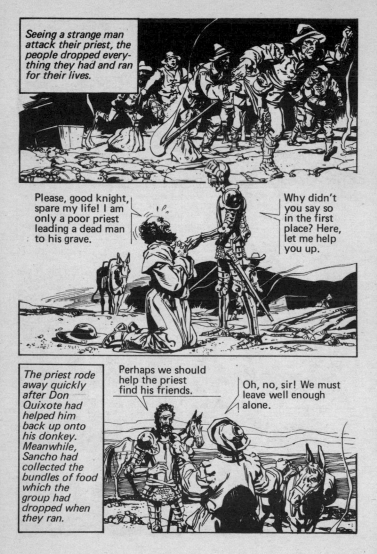

Seeing a strange man attack their priest, the people dropped everything they had and ran for their lives.

Please, good knight, spare my life! I am only a poor priest leading a dead man to his grave.

Why didn't you say so in the first place? Here, let me help you up.

The priest rode away quickly after Don Quixote had helped him back up onto his donkey. Meanwhile, Sancho had collected the bundles of food which the group had dropped when they ran.

Perhaps we should help the priest find his friends.

Oh, no, sir! We must leave well enough alone.

43

And so they rode on until they found a good place to camp.

So you see, Sancho, once again good fortune follows bad.

True, our bellies are full, but I still have no saddle for my donkey.

In the morning they rode on toward the mountains.

By and by they came upon a traveling barber who was wearing his brass shaving-bowl on his head.

Look! Do you see a knight on a grey steed? He is wearing a golden helmet!

No. I see a barber on a donkey. He is wearing a brass bowl on his head.

**Ah, Sancho! You have much to learn! That is Mambrino's golden helmet! I will win it for my own!**

**Go ahead then, Master. We never seem to see the same thing.**

*Don Quixote attacked. The poor barber jumped off his donkey and ran for cover.*

**You are not good enough to wear Mambrino's helmet!**

**Ah! I take this wonderful golden helmet as a reward for all my fighting!**

**And I take this saddle as the squire's reward!**

They rode on. Sancho was very happy with his new saddle.

I was beginning to think that being a squire would never have any rewards.

Stop! What's this?

Those are prisoners. The guards are taking them to be galley slaves.

What? That sounds wrong to me!

Halt! By whose order do you take these men against their wills to be slaves?

By the king's order. Now get out of the way.

I'll do no such thing! It is not right to take away another's freedom. I demand to know from each man why he is in chains!

46

I was in love.

I was too poor.

I sang when I should have been quiet.

These are foolish reasons. Set them free, I say!

Now it is you who are foolish. The king has ordered this. Step aside!

But Don Quixote knew what he must do.

The prisoners jumped at this chance and quickly attacked the other guards.

They even stole poor Sancho's pants.

This is the worst adventure yet! Hurry, Master, before the guards wake up and arrest us!

And so they continued toward the mountains.

I hope you don't think I'm running away because I'm afraid.

Heavens, no! It is a wise man's duty to save himself.

Finally they reached the mountains.

Ah, Sancho, now that we are here I know what I must do.

And what is that?

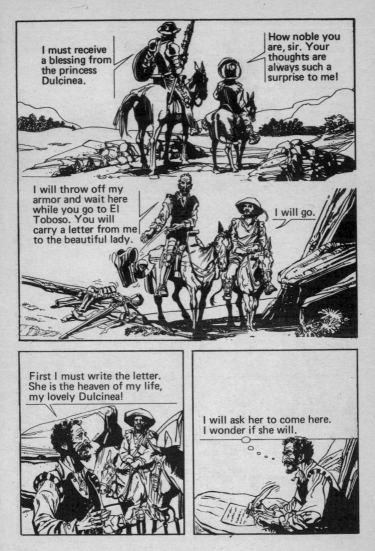

Now go, my son, and do not let yourself be dazzled by her beauty.

Sir, I don't know where her castle is, but I will do my best to find it.

*Nearing El Toboso, Sancho met a man. They spoke.*

Sir, where is the castle of princess Dulcinea?

There are no princesses and no castles in this poor little village!

*The man left, but Sancho stood thinking.*

What will I do? I can't fail my master, even though I know he is crazy! I must be a little crazy myself.

*Suddenly something he saw gave him an idea!*

*Ahead of him was the girl whom Don Quixote, in his dreams, had called the princess Dulcinea. Sancho had learned enough about magic to know what to do. So he turned and rode back quickly to Don Quixote.*

Master! Get your armor and come with me as fast as you can! The beautiful Dulcinea is out riding her horse!

*So Don Quixote got ready and rode off with Sancho as fast as he could. But when he got there, he saw only a girl on a mule!*

Sancho! Where is my beautiful Dulcinea?

Get out of my way! I'm in a hurry!

Oh, sir, it's magic! You're not seeing beautiful Dulcinea the way she really is!

*For the first time Don Quixote did not see his dreams. Instead, he saw what was really there! Sancho, however, was looking at a dream and trying not to see what was really there.*

The knight and his squire rode on. Don Quixote was sad about the strange magic. But suddenly Don Quixote pointed ahead.

Look! We may be of help there, Sancho!

A cart drawn by two horses was just in front of him.

Halt! Where are you going, and what do you carry in your cart?

It is a lion, a gift to the king. But it's been a long trip, and the lion is very hungry, so I must be on my way.

Let him out and I will show him that Don Quixote is stronger than the magic spell he is under.

It was indeed a huge lion. He stood up, turned around,

yawned,

lay back down,

and went to sleep!

Come back, lion-keeper! Anger the lion! Tease him! Make him come out!

I will not do so! Be happy, sir, that you are still alive!

Now that all was well, Sancho and the others came back.

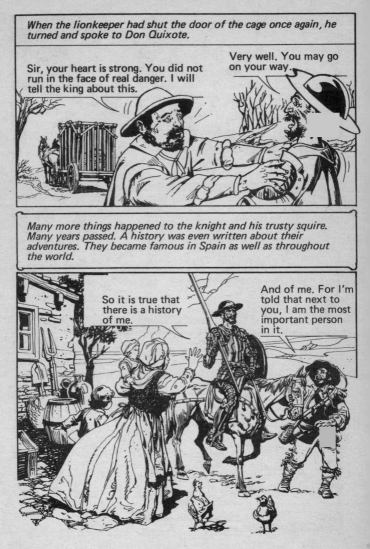

When the lionkeeper had shut the door of the cage once again, he turned and spoke to Don Quixote.

Sir, your heart is strong. You did not run in the face of real danger. I will tell the king about this.

Very well. You may go on your way.

Many more things happened to the knight and his trusty squire. Many years passed. A history was even written about their adventures. They became famous in Spain as well as throughout the world.

So it is true that there is a history of me.

And of me. For I'm told that next to you, I am the most important person in it.

*One afternoon Don Quixote saw a hunting party led by a beautiful lady. He sent Sancho with a message.*

Fair lady, Don Quixote de la Mancha would like the honor of serving you.

Go tell your master that he is welcome. My husband and I have read of his adventures.

*The duke and duchess had not only read but had also laughed at the adventures. She called her husband.*

The famous madman, Don Quixote, is coming to visit us.

*Don Quixote and Sancho galloped over to them. But as Sancho jumped off his mule, his foot caught in a strap and he fell. At this, Don Quixote stopped short and went flying over Rozinante's head.*

*It was hard for the hunting party to keep from laughing.*

After a while, they all rode on to the castle.

They entered a courtyard where six young boys helped Don Quixote off Rozinante. Then they removed his armor.

A cape was thrown across his shoulders, and he was led to the dining hall. There he feasted with the duke, the duchess, and the priest of the castle. During dinner, the duchess asked him about the spell placed on Dulcinea.

My beautiful Dulcinea still looks like a farm girl!

The duchess looked sad, but the priest spoke harshly.

You and your squire are fools to believe such things!

Don Quixote answered him solemnly.

I am not a fool. I am a knight, and I will be one until I die!

> Then the duke planned more fun.

Don Quixote, you are a good knight. To prove I respect you, I will make Sancho the governor of an island.

Kneel before the duke, Sancho! This is a great honor.

> Later Don Quixote spoke to Sancho. He told him how to act as governor.

You must be honest and always protect the poor. You must also be a little cleaner.

I'm not sure that I still want to do this!

> But Don Quixote got Sancho to go. They said goodbye, and the duke's servant took him to the island of Barataria. But the servant's job was really to make Sancho look foolish.

Sancho had to settle many arguments.

But he always showed good sense.

Then one day the servant spoke to him.

I have learned to respect you!

In spite of his good job, Sancho missed his master.

I have been governor long enough. I am leaving!

Meanwhile, although the duke and duchess had meant Don Quixote to look foolish, they looked silly themselves.

So Don Quixote and Sancho set off together again. Time passed, and many things happened to them. But one day they found themselves back at their own village.

They were met by the priest and the barber who were most happy to see them.

My friends, I have come home to stay.

As all the lives of men must come to an end, so Don Quixote, after years of adventures as a knight, finally grew sick. His niece and his housekeeper watched over him, and his good friends, the priest and the barber, often visited him. His trusty squire, Sancho Panza, never left his bedside.

My dear friends, I have been a little crazy. But now my good sense has come back. I am no longer Don Quixote de la Mancha. I know that I am Alonso Quixano, a simple man.

But the barber, the priest, and Sancho Panza wept because their friend of the wonderful dreams would no longer make life an adventure for them.

THE END

# COMPLETE LIST OF POCKET CLASSICS AVAILABLE

## CLASSICS

C 1 Black Beauty
C 2 The Call of the Wild
C 3 Dr. Jekyll and Mr. Hyde
C 4 Dracula
C 5 Frankenstein
C 6 Huckleberry Finn
C 7 Moby Dick
C 8 The Red Badge of Courage
C 9 The Time Machine
C10 Tom Sawyer
C11 Treasure Island
C12 20,000 Leagues Under the Sea
C13 The Great Adventures of Sherlock Holmes
C14 Gulliver's Travels
C15 The Hunchback of Notre Dame
C16 The Invisible Man
C17 Journey to the Center of the Earth
C18 Kidnapped
C19 The Mysterious Island
C20 The Scarlet Letter
C21 The Story of My Life
C22 A Tale of Two Cities
C23 The Three Musketeers
C24 The War of the Worlds
C25 Around the World in Eighty Days
C26 Captains Courageous
C27 A Connecticut Yankee in King Arthur's Court
C28 The Hound of the Baskervilles
C29 The House of the Seven Gables
C30 Jane Eyre
C31 The Last of the Mohicans
C32 The Best of O. Henry
C33 The Best of Poe
C34 Two Years Before the Mast
C35 White Fang
C36 Wuthering Heights
C37 Ben Hur
C38 A Christmas Carol
C39 The Food of the Gods
C40 Ivanhoe
C41 The Man in the Iron Mask
C42 The Prince and the Pauper
C43 The Prisoner of Zenda
C44 The Return of the Native
C45 Robinson Crusoe
C46 The Scarlet Pimpernel

# COMPLETE LIST OF POCKET CLASSICS AVAILABLE
(cont'd)